Mechanic Mike's Machines

Ships

A+

Smart Apple Media

Published by Smart Apple Media, an imprint of Black Rabbit Books
P.O. Box 3263, Mankato, Minnesota 56002
www.smartapplemedia.com

Produced by David West ☗ Children's Books
6 Princeton Court, 55 Felsham Road, London SW15 1AZ

Designed and illustrated by David West

Cataloging-in-Publication Data is available from the Library of Congress.
ISBN 978-1-62588-066-6

Printed in China
CPSIA compliance information: DWCB15CP
311214

9 8 7 6 5 4 3 2 1

Mechanic Mike says:
This little guy will tell you something more about the machine.

 Find out what type of engine drives the machine.

 Discover something you didn't know.

 Is it fast or slow? Top speeds are provided here.

 How many crew or people does it carry?

 Get your amazing fact here!

Contents

Sailing Ship

The earliest ships to cross the oceans were small wooden ships with sails. They were sailed by brave explorers. Sailors relied on the Sun and stars to calculate their position.

Sailing ships were powered by the wind. When at anchor, sails were pulled up and tied to the spars.

Top speed for some sailing ships was about 9 miles per hour (14.5 km/h).

The sailing ship seen here had 52 men on board.

The 18 survivors of Ferdinand Magellan's Spanish expedition (1519–1522) were the first explorers to travel around the world.

Did you know that Magellan was killed on the expedition by warriors on Mactan Island in the Philippines in 1521?

Mechanic Mike says:
In 1492, Christopher Columbus
became the first European to
sail to the West Indies and
South and Central America.

5

Mechanic Mike says:
HMS *Victory* was famous for being Lord Nelson's flagship at the Battle of Trafalgar in 1805. The ship had 104 cannons and can still be seen today at Portsmouth in England.

Warship

Because ships carrying precious cargo needed to be protected from pirates, warships and navies appeared. The most powerful warships, such as HMS *Victory*, were called men-of-war.

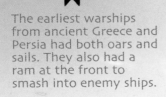

The earliest warships from ancient Greece and Persia had both oars and sails. They also had a ram at the front to smash into enemy ships.

HMS *Victory* had a crew of around 850 men.

Did you know that around 6,000 trees were used in HMS *Victory's* construction?

HMS *Victory* was powered by the wind.

HMS *Victory* had a top speed of 11 miles per hour (18 km/h).

Steamer

The steam engine provided the first mechanical power for ships. Early steam ships, like the CSS *Patrick Henry*, had large paddles on the sides to power through the water. Eventually propellers replaced paddles.

Mechanic Mike says:
In 1845 the paddle-driven HMS *Alecto* lost a tug-of-war with the propeller-driven HMS *Rattler*, showing that propellers were more efficient than paddles.

The CSS *Patrick Henry* had a crew of 150.

 Its maximum speed was around 12 miles per hour (19 km/h).

 Wooden-hulled, paddle-wheel steamships were the first steamships created to cross the Atlantic.

 Did you know that CSS *Patrick Henry* was originally called SS *Yorktown* and carried passengers and **freight** between Richmond, Virginia, and New York City?

 The CSS *Patrick Henry* was powered by a steam engine.

9

Ocean Liner

Ocean liners were the main form of transportation between distant continents until the 1960s, when plane travel became more affordable. In addition to passengers, liners like the RMS *Titanic* also carried mail and freight.

Mechanic Mike says:
The *Titanic* was considered unsinkable and had only 20 lifeboats, which were enough for just one-third of the passengers and crew.

RMS *Titanic* could carry 2,435 passengers with a crew of 892.

RMS *Titanic* had a top speed of 28 miles per hour (39 km/h).

RMS *Titanic* had 29 boilers creating steam for two steam engines and one **steam turbine**.

In 1912 the *Titanic* sank on its maiden (first) voyage after striking an iceberg. Of the 2,224 people on board, more than 1,500 died.

Did you know that ships that carried the British mail were called RMS, which stood for Royal Mail Ship?

11

Battleship

During the 18th and 19th centuries, battleships became the most powerful warships. Large armored vessels like the *Bismarck* had massive guns that could turn to face the enemy.

Mechanic Mike says:
The *Bismarck* was one of the
biggest battleships of the German
navy during World War II.
Today, battleships have been
replaced by modern weapons such
as ship-to-ship missiles.

The *Bismarck* sank
during a battle with
the British Navy
in 1941.

Did you know that
some parts of the
Bismarck's armor
was 14 inches (360
mm) thick?

The *Bismarck* had a
crew of 103 officers
and 1,962 enlisted
men.

The *Bismarck* could
travel at 34 miles per
hour (55 km/h).

The *Bismarck*
had 12 boilers
supplying steam
to three steam
turbines.

Cruise Ship

Cruise ships are built
for pleasure voyages. These
ships visit popular tourist destinations
and also have plenty of things to do
on board. These include swimming
pools, cinemas, theaters, shops,
and restaurants.

Luxurious ocean liners were often converted to cruise ships, but their high fuel use and high number of windowless cabins made them unpopular for cruising.

Enchantment of the Seas can carry 2,446 passengers.

Did you know that *Oasis of the Seas* and *Allure of the Seas* are the largest cruise ships in the world and can each carry more than 6,000 passengers?

This cruise ship can travel at 25 miles per hour (41 km/h).

Enchantment of the Seas has four **diesel-electric engines** that provide power to two electric motors. There are also bow and stern thrusters to move the ship sideways in port.

Mechanic Mike says:
Cruise ships like *Enchantment of the Seas* are like floating hotels, with staff to serve guests and to operate the ship.

Cargo Ship

Cargo ships carry goods and materials from one port to another. Bulk carriers carry coal, grain, ore, and wood in large water-tight holds. Container ships like this carry truck-size containers.

Mechanic Mike says:
Today cranes are used to place containers on board the ship. When the hull is fully loaded, additional containers are stacked on the deck. Containers are either 20 feet (6.1 m) or 40 feet (12.2 m) long.

The world's largest container ships can carry 18,000 20-foot (6.1-m) containers.

Did you know that container ships lose more than 2,500 containers at sea each year? Most go overboard during storms at sea.

This ship, the *Anna Maersk*, has a top speed of 30 miles per hour (48 km/h).

This ship has a crew of 12.

The *Anna Maersk* has a 12-cylinder **diesel engine**.

Tanker

Tankers transport liquids or gases. There are different designs for different cargoes. Tankers like this one carry crude oil. Others may carry gas in liquid form, chemicals, water, and even molasses.

Mechanic Mike says:
Oil tankers are double-hulled to prevent oil from leaking into the sea if the outer hull is damaged.

SMOKING PROHIBITED

Large tankers are called "supertankers." These ships can transport two million barrels. That's 70 million gallons (318 million liters)!

Did you know that it takes 5.5 miles (8.9 kilometers) for the largest supertankers to stop?

Oil tankers have a crew of between 15 and 24 people, depending on the size of the vessel.

Top speed on a fully-loaded oil tanker is around 20 miles per hour (32 km/h).

Supertankers are powered by the world's largest **internal combustion engines.** They are as big as a house!

19

Large, double-hulled ferries are called catamarans. They are faster than single-hulled ferries and are powered by waterjets.

Did you know that large hovercraft were once used as ferries across the English Channel? They could not operate in heavy seas.

Ferries come in all sizes. Large catamaran ferries can carry 375 passenger cars and 1,500 passengers.

The fastest ferries can travel at 54 miles per hour (87 km/h).

This ferry uses diesel engines.

Mechanic Mike says:
Some ferries can carry vehicles. This is a double-ended ferry that can shuttle between two ports without having to turn around. Cars can drive on and off both ends.

Ferry

A ferry is a ship that carries people across short distances from one port to another. Some have ramps that allow vehicles to drive on and off the vessel.

Aircraft Carrier

An aircraft carrier is a floating airbase. Military aircraft can take off and land from its deck. It is the most important ship in a navy and is protected by warships and submarines.

The USS *Enterprise* had a speed of 38 miles per hour (61 km/h).

Did you know that the USS *Enterprise* was a supercarrier? They are the largest warships ever built.

It could carry up to 90 aircraft. Aircraft were launched into the air with the help of steam-powered catapults.

The USS *Enterprise* carried 3,000 sailors, 250 pilots, and 1,500 support personnel.

The USS *Enterprise* had eight **nuclear reactors** creating steam to power four turbines.

Mechanic Mike says:
The USS *Enterprise* (CVN-65) was the world's first nuclear-powered aircraft carrier. At 1,123 feet (342 m), it was the longest naval vessel in the world.

Glossary

diesel-electric engine
A diesel engine connected to an electrical generator, which creates electricity.

diesel engine
An internal combustion engine that uses the heat of compression to ignite and burn a fuel and air mixture.

freight
Goods that are transported.

internal combustion engine
An engine where the fuel and air mixture are ignited in a combustion chamber.

nuclear reactor
A device that creates heat by a controlled nuclear chain reaction.

steam turbine
An engine where a turbine is rotated by steam.

Index